Christmas
o Sigi   1970

The Arco Book of Cats

The Arco Book of
CATS

GRACE POND

Black and white photographs by Anne Cumbers

ARCO PUBLISHING COMPANY, INC., NEW YORK

First published 1970 by Arco Publishing Company, Inc.
219 Park Avenue South, New York, N.Y. 10003.

Copyright © Text, Grace Pond, 1969

Library of Congress Catalog Number 74-89774

Standard Book Number 668-02078-4

Printed in the Netherlands and bound in Great Britain

Contents

Foreign Short-haired cats 109

Siamese 132

Pet cats 152

Acknowledgments

The Author and Publishers are especially grateful to Anne Cumbers who provided all the black-and-white photographs for this book as well as two colour plates, figures 14 and 54. They would also like to thank the following for permission to reproduce the remainder of the colour plates: Animal Photography for fig. 62; Bavaria Verlag for fig. 65; Rudolf Betz for figs. 7 and 15; Black Star Publishing Co. Ltd. for figs. 10 and 49; Camera Clix for figs. 4, 28, 31, 34, 36, 37, 45, 61, 68, 69, 78, 96, 97 and 116; Lensart/Camera Press Ltd. for figs. 29 and 112; Keystone Press Agency Ltd. for figs. 73 and 106; Kenneth Scowen for figs. 39, 40 and 66; Tivey and Hatton for fig. 76; Guy Withers for figs. 26, 72, 79, 82, 84 and 113.

Cats and kittens

The first animal with which most of us have contact is probably a cat or a kitten. When we are taught to read, the first word we proudly spell may well be 'cat'. Without realising it, we are 'cat conditioned' right from the cradle, and accept, without question, the fact that cats are an integral part of our lives.

Over recent years the status of the cat has changed. Cats are still kept on farms, in factories, and in warehouses, as killers of rats and mice, but with the modern methods for keeping down vermin, their services are not now so essential. Yet kittens are being bought in greater numbers than ever before, and although it is less than a century since keeping records of births of particular kittens was first thought of, interest has been so great that there are now more than 50 different varieties of pedigree cats. People who twenty years ago would have scoffed at the idea of paying more than a few shillings or cents for a kitten, or would even have expected to get one for nothing, now pay substantial sums for a pedigree one, without thinking twice. A person thinking of getting a new kitten may have visited a Cat Show or seen pictures of a particularly beautiful cat, and so already have in his mind a picture of what he considers is the perfect kitten for him, whether it be Siamese or Long-haired. The beautiful illustrations in this book will help anyone who is in a state of indecision. Barring accidents, cats can live very long lives, and would-be owners now realise that it is better to try and get exactly the kitten they want, as it will be their constant companion for many years to come. If you have a fancy for a particular kind of kitten but wonder if it is the one for you, visit a Cat Show, and watch them in their pens. If you see one you like, have a chat with the breeder, and if you cannot have that particular one, you may be able to order one when they are available.

I am often asked about the particular character of a specific breed, and whether I consider a kitten of this variety would make the ideal pet. In fact, this is entirely up to the owner, as the development of the kitten's character and personality will depend a great deal on the interest shown in it. If a kitten is left on its own a great deal, it will have little chance to become a real companion, and also will become quite miserable, and fed up with its own company. Before buying a kitten it is advisable to find out whether it has been inoculated against Infectious Feline Enteritis, a killer illness. If not, this should be done by a vet as soon as possible, and before it is allowed contact with other cats.

The British Cat Fancy—the cat equivalent of the Kennel Club—has a central governing and registering body, composed of delegates from the various affiliated clubs. Due to its size, the United States has several organisations, each with their own registrars, and cats may be registered with one or more, in order to be exhibited at the shows organised by the different associations. The Cat Fanciers' Association Inc. is the largest, with nearly 300 affiliated clubs. The United States has far more pedigree cats than any other country in the world, but many of their outstanding prize-winning strains have British stock in their pedigree (see p. 116). The Americans are very cat-minded and even hold an annual 'Cat Week'.

The Cat Shows in the States are run on similar lines to those on the Continent, rather than those in Britain, with the cats being taken to the judge, and the pens being hung with curtains and decorated. The Shows usually last two or three days. Although there are far more Shows in the States, the largest Cat Show in the world is the one organised in Britain by the National Cat Club and held annually in London. This is visited by many Americans who take the opportunity of buying prize-winning kittens to take back home. As there is no quarantine in the States, a kitten may be on show in London one day and in its new home the very next day, and will soon settle down.

Some thousands of pedigree cats are now registered every year. From the many famous champions, past and present, a single volume can unfortunately only portray a small selection. And in addition to the wonderful pedigree cats and kittens there are, of course, the many thousands of house pets. Whether you own a pedigree variety or a house pet and whether you prefer cats with long coats, kittens with short coats, or even the very sophisticated cats with curly coats, you will find plenty of cats to suit your fancy in the following pages.

Long-haired cats

The first domesticated cats in the British Isles had short fur and were descendants of those introduced by the Romans. It was not until the end of the sixteenth century that Long-haired cats were seen in England. These came from Turkey and Persia via France, where they were brought by travellers, who had much admired their unusual beauty. They were then referred to as Eastern Cats.

Both the Angoras (as the cats from Turkey were called) and the Persians were considered great rarities and very valuable. These Angoras were mostly white, with blue eyes, while the early Persians were frequently black or slate blue. Although the cats from both countries had long, flowing coats, there was a difference in the fur texture and in the type, and most of the Long-hairs we have today have been produced over the years by the two kinds intermating. To begin with, this was unintentional, but less than 100 years ago it was realised that, if there was to be any planned breeding, it was necessary to keep records of the cats' names. Thus pedigrees were begun. Cat Shows were held all over Britain, and those interested in cats formed clubs to promote interest in the pedigree ones. Thus the 'Cat Fancy' was started.

Mr Harrison Weir, who ran the first Cat Show at the Crystal Palace in 1871, produced his own 'Points of Excellence', which were later used as a basis for the set standards by the first registering body, the National Cat Club. Later still the Governing Council of the Cat Fancy came into being.

To return to the Long-hairs, each colour variation has its own set standard, with 100 points allocated for what would be a perfect specimen. The points given for the different characteristics may vary slightly between each variety; for example, the head of the Blue Persian has 25 points, while the head of Black has 20, more being given for the coat colour in the latter case.

The ideal Long-hair should have a very broad round head, with good width between the small tufted ears. The cheeks should be full and round, the nose short and broad, and the eyes round and large. The coat is very important, and should be soft, silky, and very dense, and never woolly in texture. The tail should be short and full, a kink or break being considered a defect, which may cause disqualification if the cat was shown. The body should be cobby on low sturdy legs. The fur around the head should be brushed up to form a soft frame for the face.

A cat conforming in every way to all these requirements would doubtless have the makings of an outstanding champion, but, even if the nose of a kitten is a shade too long, it still has a natural elegance and beauty, and makes a most decorative pet. A kitten must be four months old before it may be exhibited in the United States, but whereas in Britain it is not considered an adult until nine months old, in America it can enter the class for cats when only eight months old. It may become a Champion at an earlier age, and as points are given to the winner of the Champion class, according to the number of other champions beaten, if a very good cat, it may soon get the hundred points required and bear the much-sought-after title of Grand Champion before its name.

Cats with the same coloured fur all over are known as the self-colours. Under this category comes the Blacks, the Whites, the Blues, the Creams, and the very rare Reds. The Tabbies, Brown, Silver and Red in colour should have a clearly defined pattern of markings. The Chinchilla is a ticked cat, while the Blue Cream should have these two colours intermingled in the coat. The Colourpoint and Birman have Siamese colourings, while the Tortoiseshells and the Tortoiseshell-and-Whites are known as the patched cats. Any cat not answering to any standard may be registered as 'Any Other Variety'.

The Long-haired varieties recognised in the States, which until recently far outnumbered all other pedigree varieties, are very much the same as in Britain. There are a few more colour variations; one such variety being the Cameo, with cream coloured fur, red tipped. For more than 100 years, Maine has had its Coon cats. These have thick and longish fur, with coats of many colours, and resulted through the interbreeding of the cats arriving on ships from all over the world. The coats are said to resemble those of the racoons, and before it was realised that this was quite impossible they were thought to have originated as a result of cats mating with racoons.

Long-haired   BLACK

The young kitten in figure 1 shows great promise and illustrates the difference between the coat of a fully-grown cat and that of a kitten, as it is often not until the adult stage is reached that the true shining black lustrous coat may be seen. Usually, when young, the kittens have grey, even rusty brown coats, with many white hairs, and before now have been mistaken for Smokes, another Long-haired variety. Even in the black and white photographs it is easy to spot the difference between the fur of the kitten and that of the gorgeous fully-grown cat in figure 2. The eye contrast too is striking. Kittens are born blind, with the eyes of long-coated varieties not opening until they are about nine to ten days old. They are then blue in colour, and take some weeks to change gradually to deep copper or orange.

Black kittens may appear in litters from Tortoiseshells and Tortoiseshell-and-Whites, as well as from two black parents. It is interesting to realise that some of the best Black bred have had a Blue Persian parent. Black males may be used in the breeding of Whites, Smokes, Tortoiseshell, Tortoiseshell-and-Whites, and Bi-Colours.

To many a black cat is a sign of good luck, and there are countless superstitions connected with them. They are particularly beloved by sailors, being supposed to bring good luck to the ship, but in some parts of Germany they are considered to bring bad, not good fortune.

Although Black Long-hairs are one of the oldest recognised varieties, having appeared at the early Cat Shows, they are still comparatively few in number. But they make up in quality what they lack in quantity.

Careful breeding has produced some superb Black champions, with jet black glossy coats and enormous round orange eyes, and these attract much attention at the Shows.

As may be imagined, grooming plays an important part in producing these prize-winning Blacks, and before they are shown many weeks of hard work are necessary on the part of the owner to make sure the coat will be as perfect as possible. Even hot sunshine or extreme damp may cause the fur to take on a brownish hue, which would be faulted by the judge. Ideally the fur should be absolutely black right down to the roots, and there must be no white hairs anywhere. Brushing and combing are vital to make sure there are no old hairs left in the coat, and polishing with a chamois leather or a piece of silk will help to give the coat that much-admired sheen. Some breeders advocate sprinkling on a few drops of bay rum and then polishing with a piece of velvet when the fur has dried. A champion must not only conform as nearly as possible to the required standard, but when judged it must be in absolutely tip-top condition: every hair should stand away from the body, the corners of the sparkling eyes should be free from dirt, and the inside of the ears quite clean.

Even if not show specimens, Blacks make delightful pets. They appear to be particularly intelligent, and very fond of their owners. I know, as I owned one for years.

1   *Black Long-haired kitten*

2   *Ch. Coylum Black Pearl*

3 *Mrs Pearson's White kitten*

Long-haired WHITE (BLUE EYES)

The first cats with long coats seen in Europe appear to have been white coated with blue eyes. Old books refer to them as the original Angoras, and the fur was said to be long, silky and clinging, but, because nothing was known about grooming, the coat was sometimes 'dusky white' rather than 'whiter than white'. These early Angoras had long noses and upright ears— faults still affecting many of this variety today, at least in Europe. In North America some very good specimens can be found, with short noses and small rounded ears, which is really what the standard requires. But in Britain they are still one of the rarest breeds, although Whites with orange eyes are increasing in numbers all the time. Unfortunately, right from the earliest days, it was discovered that blue-eyed White cats, whether long or short-coated, have a tendency to deafness. A black smudge on the forehead, or some black hairs in the coat are looked on as good signs by breeders, as frequently these kittens have good hearing.

A typical example of a blue-eyed White kitten may be seen in figure 4. All kittens are born with blue eyes, but they can change as they grow. If, however, the eyes are still a good blue when they reach the age of three months, they will probably stay that colour. To improve the type, cross-mating with those with orange eyes is often tried. This may result in 'odd-eyed' kittens being born, that is with one blue eye and one orange. These 'odd-eyes' are very useful when endeavouring to produce good Blue-eyed Whites. They usually have good or at least partial hearing.

As with all Long-hairs, daily grooming plays an important part in making these cats look immaculate. Talcum powder brushed well into the fur will help to remove any grease marks. Frequently yellow stains appear at the base of the tail, which may need shampooing to remove. Indeed, many owners bath their Whites a few days before they are to appear at a show, but great care has to be taken when doing this, to make sure they do not go out before the fur is thoroughly dry, as all cats are very susceptible to draughts and may catch cold.

The kittens are very pink when first born, but the fur grows rapidly, and in a matter of weeks, they become adorable bundles of white fluff. The particularly strong appeal of white cats and kittens can be gauged by their frequent appearances in both press and television advertising.

Long-haired WHITE (ORANGE EYES)

Whites with orange eyes first appeared as the result of trying to improve the type of those with blue eyes, but they were so much admired, that they were soon granted recognition in their own right, i.e. were given a separate standard of their own. Today they may be regarded as one of the most popular of the Long-hairs.

Modern breeders have worked really hard and have by careful breeding

produced outstanding specimens, which often win the coveted title of 'Best in Show'. Whereas once the Whites in other parts of the world were much better than the British, the latter are now as good, if not better. How good that is may well be seen in the photograph of Ch. Coylum Marcus (6). He was awarded the title of 'British Ambassador' by an American Cat Club. The two kittens owned by Mrs Stevens and featured in figure 5 bear prefixes 'Snowhite' and 'Charmina' which are internationally famous.

Whites may be obtained from Black matings, as well as from Whites, Blues, even from Creams. They are also useful to breed from when endeavouring to produce Tortoiseshell-and-Whites.

Many people would like to own a White kitten, but feel a little worried about the time needed to keep such a pet looking immaculate. But in fact they are not much more trouble than any other cat with long fur, as grooming is necessary for them all, particularly in the late autumn and spring when the old hairs must be brushed and combed out. Perhaps the White's paws get

5 Long-haired Whites, owned by Mrs Stevens

6 *Miss Sellars' Ch. Coylum Marcus*

more muddy-looking than other cats', but these can soon be wiped dry, and after a sprinkling of talcum powder a quick brush will restore them to their former beauty. Most Whites seem to take a pride in their appearance, spend hours washing, and with a little daily attention from their owners are always a decorative addition to any household.

The White featured in figure 7 shows the eye colour and shape, also the rounded ears, and the pink tip to the nose, a delightful feature of this variety.

Long-haired   BLUE

Although the first cats with long fur were known to have come from Turkey
(hence the name Angora or Ankara cats), others soon followed from Persia.
The coat texture appears to have differed from that of the Angora, being not
so silky or clinging, and, although the two varieties have been interbred
over the years, it is still possible to distinguish between the two fur types.
Mention is made in the early cat books of the Black Persian, and this was
said to be the most valuable, with the slate or blue colour being next. The first
Cat Show was not held until 1871, when a number of cats with blue fur
were shown, and were much admired. However, old photographs show very
little comparison between these early Blues and the outstanding ones we
have today. The first exhibits very rarely had sound blue coats. Often they
had white patches, even tabby markings, and green eyes. Careful planned
breeding has now brought the Blues near to perfection, that is to the 100
points required to comply with the set standard. Although any shade of blue
is permitted, the fur must be the same even colour throughout, with the
paler shades being preferred.

   Because of the outstanding type and good orange eye colour, Blues are
frequently used to improve the type and eyes of other varieties, such as
Blacks. They are also used in the breeding of Blue Creams.

   The kittens are full of fun, and from about the age of three weeks will be
climbing out of their box, and even at this early age, should be given a toilet
tray to use. All varieties of kittens, whether Long- or Short-haired, will
very soon become house-trained given the opportunity. At this age too, just
a minute or two's daily grooming will get them used to being handled. The
hair should be gently brushed up all around the head to form a frill which
will eventually frame the face. Figures 8 and 10 illustrate very well typical
Blues, with broad heads, neat ears, firm chins and big orange eyes, while the
delightful kittens in the hat picture (9), only a few weeks old, also show the
same features, although their eye colour is still changing.

9   *Mrs Grace Pond's Bluestar kittens*

11 Deebank Ruby, Red Self

Long-haired RED SELF

This is one of the rarer varieties, not only in Britain, but in most parts of the world where there is a growing cat fancy. The colour should be a deep rich mahogany red, very striking when even all over with no stripes or lighter hairs. Red Selfs were originally bred from lightly marked Red Tabbies and it has proved exceedingly difficult to breed a cat that is entirely a Self Red. Most have stripes somewhere; the face being invariably marked with a tabby pattern, and the tail ringed. The type is good, the nose being short, the copper-coloured eyes big and round, and the head round, with small ears.

The few exhibited are most attractive, as may be seen from the picture of the Pathfinder kitten bred by Miss Woodifield (12), and that of the adult cat bred by Miss Bull (11). Both are now owned by Miss E. Sellars. A cat with a rich red coat and no markings would be most useful in the breeding of Tortoiseshells and Tortoiseshell-and-Whites.

Red kittens are alert and vivacious, and for some reason seem to appeal particularly to men. It is popularly supposed that all red cats, whether self-coloured or tabby, must be males, but litters from all-red parentage may contain both male and female kittens. If not pure bred, there may be Tortoiseshell females and Red males in the litter.

It is advisable not to buy a kitten under 9–10 weeks of age, for by then, it should be fully weaned, used to mixed feeding, and house-trained. A kitten of this age requires about four small meals a day, to include raw or cooked meat (preferably beef), cooked fish (white, without bones), rabbit, chicken, heart, and a little liver. A few cornflakes or some brown bread may be added. Water should always be left down, and cow's milk given very sparingly at first, as some kittens cannot take it. A baby cereal can be mixed with a little milk.

12 Pathfinder Red Self kitten

Long-haired   CREAM

Startops Twinkletoes (13), a beautiful Cream bred by Mrs King and owned by Mrs Shepard, finds the whole business of being photographed exceedingly boring, hence the very wide yawn.

One of the most popular of the Long-hairs, this variety was referred to as 'Fawn' when first shown in the 1890s. They appeared by accident from cross-matings, possibly from Tortoiseshells, and were largely ignored at first. It was many years before breeders were able to produce kittens with the lovely 'Devonshire cream' coats now seen today.

Many of the best Creams have been bred from Blues, as it has been found that Cream mated to Cream indefinitely may result in loss of type. A bad fault is for the colour to be what is referred to as 'Hot', that is when the fur is more red than cream. Faint bars or markings would also be faulted by a judge. The cat in figure 15 is very dark by comparison with the lovely Creams

29

14 *Pensford Cream kittens*

now seen, but he is a wonderful looking animal, and certainly a massive cat.

Creams play an important part in the breeding of the increasingly popular, but invariably female, Blue Cream (for further details see p. 34).

The pair of Pensford kittens (14) bred by Mrs J. Thompson are outstanding examples of what a would-be buyer of a future champion should look for when buying a cream kitten. The colour is pure, even all over; the heads are broad and round, with neat ears, and they have cobby bodies on sturdy legs. Even at the early age of eight weeks, the copper eye colour is appearing. All kittens are naturally photogenic, although much patience is needed to catch them in really striking poses, as in figure 16.

Kittens need exercise to keep them happy and healthy. Running after balls, even fighting and playing with one another will provide this, and is very amusing to watch, but kittens should never be regarded as playthings,

30

particularly by young children. Their bones are very soft, and even squeezing too hard can result in damage to the ribs.

Startops Honeybunch belonging to Mrs L. Shepard is an excellent example of an adult Cream, showing good type, big round eyes, and even colour. The picture (17) shows clearly how important grooming is to keep the long pale cream fur looking immaculate. Also note the fine set of whiskers. These are very important to a cat, being connected with nerves, and acting as sensitive organs of perception.

17   Startops Honey Bunch, owned by Mrs Shepard

6   Mrs Thompson's Cream kittens at play

Long-haired BLUE CREAM

More and more breeders are interested in Blue Creams because of the several variations it is possible to have in the litters they produce. And, apart from being a most attractive variety, they also appear to be very intelligent, and definitely cats of character.

The variety is invariably female, any males born proving sterile. The result of Blue and Cream cross-matings, the type is usually very good. The recognised standard in Britain says that the long silky coat should be of the pastel shades of blue and cream, softly intermingled, giving a shot-silk effect. This is quite difficult to achieve, and often there are some cream patches, and sometimes a solid coloured paw. A cream mark on the head, referred to as a blaze, is permitted. In North America, the Blue Creams may be patched, rather than intermingled, which is much easier to produce. Although the first Blue Creams were produced more or less as the result of accidental breeding, geneticists soon worked out a definite formula, as follows:

A Blue Cream mated to a Blue could have Blue males, Cream males, Blue females or Blue Cream females.

A Blue Cream mated to a Cream could have Blue males, Cream males, Cream females or Blue Cream females.

A Cream female mated to a Blue male could have Blue Cream females or Cream males.

A Blue female mated to a Cream male could have Blue Cream females or Blue males.

Blue Creams have also been known to appear in litters from Tortoiseshells.

The Pensford kittens (18) illustrate well how the cross-breeding works out, the one on the left being a Blue Cream and the other a Cream. The father was a Cream and the mother a Blue Cream. Fiesta, the little Blue Cream kitten, is an excellent example of all that is required by the standard. She has good type, big round eyes, and a well intermingled coat. In fact, since this picture was taken, she has been a 'Best in Show' kitten.

Coylum Anne, an adult Blue Cream, shows clearly the cream blaze on the head. Hers is slightly bigger than usual, but most breeders feel it adds character to the face.

34

18 *Pensford Blue Cream and Cream kittens*

19   Coylum Anne, Blue Cream

20 *Smoke, owned by Mrs Smith*

Long-haired SMOKE

This is one of the most striking of all varieties of pedigree cats. At first glance, a Smoke may be mistaken for a Black, but as it moves intriguing glimpses of the silky white undercoat may be seen, and a second glance reveals a black mask to the face, enhanced by the silver ear tufts and full silver frill. It is referred to quite correctly in the set standard as 'a cat of contrasts'.

Although this is one of the oldest varieties, being first recognised as long ago as 1893, comparatively few are seen at Shows, which is a great pity, as a good Smoke is most distinctive. There are two colour variations, the Black and the Blue.

How the breed first started seems rather a mystery. Some say that it originated from poorly marked Silver Tabbies, while others think that various cross-matings between Blues, Blacks, Shaded Silvers and Chinchillas produced the first Smoke. Whatever their origin, they are still difficult to breed. A Smoke mated to another Smoke may produce good Smoke kittens, but this is not always so. Some breeders use a Black stud with very good results, although it is not always easy to know at first whether the kittens are Blacks or Smokes, as some black kittens have a smokey appearance until the adult stage is reached. Many are registered as Smokes, and then turn out to have wonderful black coats when they are older.

The Blue Smoke has the distinctive colour contrast, but blue replaces the black, and from the distance the cat may be mistaken for a Blue. When walking the white undercoat may be seen. The frill and ear tufts should be white, and the mask of the face blue. Both varieties should have large round copper or orange colour eyes, and to be really striking the frill should be extra long.

The intriguing photograph below (21) shows Black and Blue Smoke kittens when only two and three weeks old (though the one on the extreme end is possibly a young Black). These are Kala kittens bred by Miss Collins, and illustrate well how the white undercoat gradually appears through the dark top coat, but it will be many months before their appearance equals that of the adult (20), owned by Miss Smith.

21   *Smokes and Black kittens, bred by Miss Collins*

22   Kala Smoke and Black kittens

Smokes are one of the most difficult cats to present to perfection on the show bench. Indeed I have heard their owners say that they are really at their best only two months in the year. Hot sunshine gives the fur a rusty tinge, while rain and damp makes it even more brownish and clinging as well. Then there is the difficulty of knowing whether to use talcum powder on the fur. It is ideal for the white undercoat, removing the grease and making it springy to the touch, but great care has to be taken to make sure that there is none on the black tips, or on the face. Any powder left in a cat's coat when it is being shown may mean disqualification by the judge.

Smoke kittens are known for their amusing characters. They behave like clowns, always getting into mischief and inquisitive about anything new, as may be seen by the little Smoke in figure 22 which was very intrigued when first presented with a ball.

39

Long-haired TABBIES

Although many cats have tabby markings on their fur, not many people realise that pedigree varieties should conform to a specified pattern. It has been claimed that if all the domestic cats in the world were allowed to inter-mate freely, they would eventually all have tabby markings. This I can well believe, as even in cross-matings with pedigree cats a Brown Tabby turns up in the litter. In spite of this, it is exceedingly difficult to breed a cat whose markings conform exactly to the pattern required. In the Long-hairs, the flowing coats make the pattern less easy to see.

Whatever the background colour of the coat, the tabby markings should be distinct as possible. It is easier to see this pattern if one looks down on the cat. From this position the stripes and bars around the shoulders should resemble butterfly wings. The cheeks should have delicate swirlings, and there should be lines forming spectacles around the eyes. A thick vertical line should run down the spine flanked on each side by a parallel thinner line. Both the tail and the legs should be ringed. There should be two rings, like necklaces, on the chest. These are referred to as 'Lord Mayor's chains'. The 'M' on the forehead and the delicate pencillings on the face may be distinctly seen in Mrs Greenwood's Silver Tabby Champion Wilmar Wendy (24).

Long-haired SILVER TABBY

Early Cat Show catalogues show that the Silver Tabby classes were usually well filled, but the reports on the cats entered make it clear that they would stand very little chance of winning a first prize, if shown today. Often the markings were quite indistinct, running into one another and forming a solid black back. The background colour, which is one of the features of this variety and which should be a pure pale silver, was often more blue than anything.

Over the years carefully planned breeding on the part of dedicated cat lovers has resulted in most attractive animals, as may be seen in the delightful picture of the kittens bred by Mrs Greenwood (23). Many Silver Tabbies now have long dense silky coats of pale silver, contrasting well with the jet-black markings, and the green or hazel round eyes.

Silver Tabbies are said to have been used to produce the fairy-like Chinchillas, their close relations the Shaded Silvers (not recognised in Britain) and the Smokes. Of course, faults still appear in the shape of brown tinges in the fur and blurred markings. This is known as brindling and is caused by some of the light background hairs appearing in the dark markings.

The kittens when first born are usually dark, with the silver background only appearing as the fur grows. Grooming is essential to make the coat stand up and to display the tabby markings to the best advantage. Grooming is important to all cats, but even more particularly to the Long-hairs, as daily brushing and combing will rid the coat of old hairs, which otherwise the cat would lick down, and this could cause what is known as a fur ball. This is one of the reasons why a cat should always have access to grass, either in the garden or grown in a pot indoors. Grass acts as a natural emetic, and any fur swallowed will be sicked up. A weekly dose of vegetable oil, such as corn oil, will also help to prevent this.

23   *Mrs Greenwood's Long-haired Silver Tabby kittens*   24   *Ch. Wilmar Wendy, Silver Tabby*

Long-haired BROWN TABBY

The first Long-haired Tabby mentioned in the old cat books seems to have been a Brown Tabby from Russia. The cat featured was a despondent-looking animal, with shaggy coat and very little tabby markings, but it is interesting to note that it had large orange-coloured eyes. It may well have been responsible for the lovely eye colour we have today, as many of the earlier cats were said to have green eyes.

The first Angoras and Persians were self-coloured, that is the fur was the same colour all over, but there were many native Short-haired Tabbies. These were probably used to introduce the correct pattern of markings into the long-coated cats.

There are still very few Brown Tabbies exhibited at the Shows today, and these often fail in type, that is to say the nose may be a shade too long, or the ears too big. The difficulty is to find suitable studs that will improve the type, without losing the correct markings, and I have only seen one or two really outstanding ones during the past few years. Blacks have been tried as sires, but these may introduce too solid markings.

A good Brown Tabby should have a full long coat of rich tawny sable, with the markings a definite black (25). Often the coat is not a distinct black and the markings are smudged. The kitten featured in figure 26 has good type, but by show standards his coat would be considered far too pale.

25 Mrs Pearson's Brown Tabby Long-hair

26 Long-haired Tabby

Long-haired RED TABBY

The colour of the Red Tabby pedigree cat should be a deep rich red. Rich red is essential, as there often is some confusion with pets with sandy coloured coats, as many believe that this is the colour required. At early Cat Shows, they were referred to as 'Orange', as this was then the best description of the colour; but over the years breeders have managed to produce cats with almost mahogany-coloured fur. The pattern of markings should be an even deeper, darker red, and it can prove quite difficult to breed cats with the correct markings, standing out quite clearly from the background. The type in many cases is now very good, that is the noses are short, the ears small and well-rounded, and the heads broad. Mrs Rosell's Ch. Bruton Paisano (27) is an excellent example of the modern Red Tabby. He, like all cats, loves to doze in the warm sunshine.

Many of the Reds are males, massive in size. These have often been born from Tortoiseshells, but it is not true to say that all Red Tabbies are males. When both parents have pure red breeding, there may be both male and female kittens in the litter. Apart from pale-coloured coats, other faults may be white under the chin, on the chest, or a white tip to the tail.

Red males are sometimes used as mates for Tortoiseshells and Tortoiseshell-and-Whites, as both the last-named are all-female varieties, but there is always the danger that tabby markings may be introduced, which could be difficult to breed out, and may even appear in future generations.

Even if a Ginger, rather than Red, the delightful kitten in figure 28 would always make a very ornamental pet, and would repay many times over all the love and care bestowed on it. It is unfair to buy a young kitten and leave it alone all day, as its house-training will be neglected, which could turn it into a dirty cat. A kitten also needs at least four small meals a day, and food should not be left down, particularly in hot weather when it may become contaminated by flies. Each meal should be put down fresh, and the kitten allowed about ten minutes to eat it, any left overs being removed. If the kitten appears to be ravenous, but is still on the thin side, worms should be suspected, and the vet consulted as to the correct treatment. A young kitten should never be wormed out indiscriminately. More kittens have probably died that way than have died through having worms.

29 *Chinchilla*

28 *Long-haired Marmalade*

Long-haired   CHINCHILLA

This is a cat that always attracts admiring glances and comments on its beauty. They are not a new variety as sometimes supposed, but appeared at Shows as long ago as the 1890s. In a book on cats published in 1894, John Jennings, the author, says: 'The Chinchilla is a peculiar but beautiful variety; the fur at the roots is silver, and shades to the tips to a decided slate hue, giving a most pleasing and attractive appearance.'

The early Chinchillas were produced from Blue breeding, and would today be referred to as Blue Chinchilla. These are not yet recognised and would appear in the 'Any Other Variety' classes. The first Chinchillas with their silver black-tipped fur are said to have been bred from Silver Tabbies. Some were more heavily ticked than others, and were known as the Shaded Silvers. The judges at the beginning of the century found it difficult to distinguish a heavily ticked Chinchilla from a lightly ticked Shaded Silver, and at one Show the same cat received a prize from one judge as being one variety, and from another judge as being the other! Eventually Chinchillas alone were recognised in Britain, but the Shaded Silvers are still exhibited on the Continent and other parts of the world.

Slightly lighter in bone (but by no means delicate) than some of the other Long-hairs, the light-black ticking on the pure white undercoat gives a Chinchilla an almost sparkling appearance. The type is as for other Long-hairs, but a distinctive feature is the eyes, emerald or blue-green in colour, with their black or brown rims. The nose tip should be a brick-red. The beauty of the eyes and the long flowing coat shows up well in the picture (30) of the boy with his much-loved, and very decorative, pet.

The kittens are very dark when first born, and on seeing them it is hard to imagine the faint tabby markings and shadow rings on the tails they often have will ever disappear, but they soon vanish as the fur grows.

Whatever attitude they adopt, Chinchillas cannot help being photogenic, and for this reason appear in many press and TV advertisements.

Long-haired TORTOISESHELL

Tortoiseshells are regarded by some as the most fascinating of all cats, with their coats of black, red and cream. They are referred to as patched cats, and each colour of this patching should be entirely distinct from the other with the cream and red being as bright as possible. The paws, as well as the body, should have patches of colour, and this is referred to as 'broken', even the ears should have tiny patches. A blaze of red or cream is liked on the face: this is a mark running down from the forehead. Many breeders consider it adds character to the face, but it is not insisted on in the set standard.

As Tortoiseshells are invariably female, any males born proving to be sterile, choosing a mate can be quite a problem. A good choice would probably be a stud of one of the coat colour, i.e. cream, black or red, or one of the newly-recognised Bi-Colours. Even so, it is not possible yet to breed Tortoiseshells to order, and the resultant litter may contain a wonderful multi-coloured selection of kittens, including even a Blue Cream. Tortoiseshells are found on farms quite frequently, but then they are more or less an accident of birth, and arrive through indiscriminate mating among a number of cats of different hues and coat patterns. They are, of course, not pedigree.

Many of the pedigree Tortoiseshells are rather sombre in appearance, having too much black in the coat. The ideal cat should have a coat of bright patches of red and cream, evenly interspersed with the black. The coat should be long and flowing and needs to be well brushed up, to allow the colouring to be seen to its best advantage. Due to cross-breeding, the type of those seen at recent shows has been very good. A good pair—mother and daughter—

50

belonging to Mrs Shepard appear in figure 32. Show preparation is very important, but apart from grooming, any would-be exhibitors should remember that it is also important to ensure that a cat has clean ears. A gentle wipe inside the ears with slightly dampened cotton wool should remove any dirt or dust, but if there are signs of a discharge, it may be caused by a canker mite, and a vet should be consulted as to the correct treatment. Ear trouble can result in a cat being refused admission to a Show, as every exhibit has to be examined by a vet before it is allowed to be penned.

52

Long-haired TORTOISESHELL-AND-WHITE

This is a variety closely allied to the Tortoiseshells. It should have the same coloured patches, with the addition of white. The patches should be of red, cream and black distributed all over the body, well interspersed with white—but not too much white. This is another all-female variety, and for anyone interested in breeding from the queen (this is the name given to a pedigree female cat once she is old enough for mating) a wise choice would be a

33 Pathfinder Tortie-and-White kitten

self-coloured male of one of the colours in the coat. It is very difficult to produce a kitten with the correct patched coat. The Tortie-and-White kitten in figure 34 is adorable, but the coat could be more definitely patched. However, it is difficult enough even to breed Tortoiseshell-and-White kittens, let alone produce them with correct patching, though one English breeder through sticking to certain strains has been most successful with this. Many others have tried for years, experimenting with various matings, but have been unsuccessful.

There is a quite erroneous belief that any male Tortoiseshell-and-White is worth a fortune. As I have said before, there are a few born, but invariably they prove sterile, and I can find no proof of one that has actually sired any kittens. Several of those who are said to have sired kittens turn out, on inspection, to have tabby or other markings on them, and are not genuine Tortie-and-Whites at all.

Because there are so few kittens of this variety, I am always getting enquiries for them. They are most attractive, very intelligent and forward for their age. The Pathfinders kitten (33) is only four weeks old, but already very self-reliant and demanding attention. Litters from Tortie-and-Whites will certainly be many coloured, and may contain Bi-Colours, Blacks, Reds, Blue Creams, and if very lucky, Tortoiseshells and Tortoiseshell-and-Whites. In America, both the Long-haired and the Short-haired Tortoiseshell-and-Whites are referred to as the Calicos.

34 Long-haired Tortoiseshell-and-White kitten

Long-haired BI-COLOURED

Bi-Colours are often the result of two self-coloured cats mating, or they may appear in litters from Tortoiseshells and Tortoiseshell-and-Whites. Cats with coats of two colours were entered at the early Cat Shows, those with black and white fur being referred to as 'Magpie'.

They have recently received re-recognition in Britain, but the standard which has been approved is the old one, i.e. the colours should be entirely distinct from one another and the markings should resemble those of a Dutch rabbit. It is terribly difficult to breed a cat or kitten with such a coat pattern, and frequently the challenge certificates have been withheld. The colours may be black, blue, red or cream, all with white, the type being as for other Long-hairs—see the Bi-Colour bred by Miss Woodifield (35).

Many readers may not realise just how difficult it is to become a Champion. A cat may not compete in adult classes until at least nine months old, and cannot be entered in the Open class, for which 'challenge certificates' are given, before this age.

An Open class is the breed class, and if considered up to the standard, the winner of such a class may be granted a challenge certificate by the judge. If it is not considered good enough, the judge may decide to withhold the challenge certificate, but another judge must also agree to this. If a cat wins three challenge certificates at three shows under three different judges, the Governing Council of the Cat Fancy will check this, and after verification, the cat may bear the much-sought-after title of 'Champion' before its name. For a male this may mean an increase in the demand for his services as a stud; and for a female, her kittens will be in great demand, as coming from champion stock, and very useful in further breeding.

Long-haired   ANY OTHER COLOUR

Cats or kittens which answer to no recognised standard, or may result from mis-matings, cross-breedings, or possibly from experimental breedings when a breeder is endeavouring to produce a new variety, may be registered under the category of 'Any Other Colour' As all cats must be registered before being exhibited at shows held under the jurisdiction of the Governing Council of the Cat Fancy, this allows such cats to be entered. However, as they do not have a set standard (for they do not conform to the given characteristics), they cannot compete for challenge certificates and can never become

37   Kittens of Any Other Colour

champions. Of course, if they are a new variety which eventually is given a standard, they could then be re-registered and may compete for challenge certificates.

To produce a new variety is not at all easy. It can take years, and will mean many of the kittens having to be sold cheaply as not up to standard or given away as pets. The characteristics or the new colour required may not be easy to fix, and in any case there must be at least three generations of pure breeding before any thought can be given to applying for a standard and a breed number.

The kittens in figure 37 show how attractive 'Any Other Colour' can be.

Long-haired COLOURPOINT

This is an excellent example of a man-made variety, which was produced only after many years of patient and selective breeding. Colourpoints are long-coated cats, bearing the distinctive Siamese coat pattern: the main body colour is light and the points (the legs, tails, mask of the face and the ears) are dark. They are not Siamese with long fur, but definitely Long-hairs, having the short noses, the big round eyes, the broad heads and neat ears typical of the Long-haired type. They were produced in the first place by mating Siamese with self-coloured Long-hairs, but the Siamese type has now been cleverly bred out. Great difficulty was experienced by the early breeders in retaining the bright blue eye colour of the Siamese, without losing the big round eyes so much admired in the Long-haired varieties. This has been achieved, but some of the Colourpoints do fail a little on eye colour.

As with the Siamese, it has been found possible to have several variations of the point colouring, and, although the originals had Seal-points, Blue, Chocolate and Lilac are now being bred.

When young, the kittens are cream-coated, with little pink noses and blue eyes, and in a very short time, the point colouring starts to appear, as may be seen in the photograph of the kittens bred by Mrs Hann (38). The eyes may deepen in colour as the kittens grow older, and it may take 18 months for the full adult colouring of the points to be reached. While a small kink is permitted in the tail of a Siamese, it would definitely be a defect in a Colourpoint.

60

The numbers of Colourpoints are increasing all the time, both in Britain and in North America, where they are known as Himalayans. They are exported all over the world from Great Britain.

Champion Niobe Shere Khan (41) is an excellent example of what is required. He is a Seal-point and has very good dark points, excellent type, big round eyes, and neat small ears. Handsome specimens of both kittens and an adult may be seen in figures 39 and 40.

38   Colourpoint kittens bred by Mrs Hann

40 *Colourpoint kittens*

39 *Long-haired Colourpoint*

Long-haired BIRMAN

Although this variety has been known and exhibited on the Continent since the 1930s, it has only recently been seen in Britain, and now has a recognised standard.

It differs from all other pedigree cats in that the paws should be pure white, like little gloves, with those on the back legs extending into a point up the legs.

The colouring is that of the Siamese and the Colourpoints, except for the white feet. The body colouring has a slightly golden tinge rather than cream, contrasting well with the dark points. As may be seen from the photographs of those owned by Mrs E. Fisher (42 and 43), the head is slightly longer than that of the Colourpoint, as is also the body, while the bushy tail is not quite so short as that of the other Long-hairs. It has now been found possible to produce them with point colours other than Seal.

Legend has it that the Birmans are descended from the sacred cats of Burma, which once guarded the temples, while another story, more prosaic, says that they originated through a white-footed Siamese mating with a Long-hair.

The kittens are delightful, treading daintily around on their little white paws. They are light-coloured when born, the points deepening with age.

The first seen in England were imported from France, and this meant that they had to spend six months in quarantine. There are very stringent laws covering the importation of a cat or kitten into Britain. Permission has to

42 Mrs E. Fisher's Birman kitten

43   Orlamonde de Khlaramoor, Birman

be obtained from the Ministry of Agriculture, Hook Rise, Tolworth, Surrey, and arrangements made well in advance. The animal will be met at the airport or ship by an approved carrying agent and taken direct to the quarantine station. The six-month quarantine is necessary to ensure that no rabies is introduced into the country. Cats, as well as dogs, foxes and other animals, are susceptible to this disease, but the solitary confinement is particularly hard on them. The owner is permitted to visit frequently during the permitted visiting hours. This should be done as often as possible.

There are now a number of recommended quarantine establishments, and a list of these, together with the rules and regulations governing quarantine, may be obtained from the Ministry of Agriculture.

British Short-haired cats

These are pedigree Short-hairs which have been developed over the years from the original domesticated cats. The name 'British' is given to distinguish them from those of supposedly Foreign origin. The colour variations and coat patterns are almost the same as those of the Long-hairs. The characteristics of the Britishers are entirely opposite to those of the 'Foreigners' such as the Siamese. They are frequently referred to as square cats, as the bodies should be sturdy, with full chests, on strong well-proportioned legs; the heads round, with good width between the slightly rounded ears. The cheeks should be well developed, and the chins firm. The tails should be thick at the base, and the length in proportion to the body, never too long. The fur should be short, fine and close, never woolly. They should be strong muscular-looking cats.

The eye colour may differ according to the variety, but they should be large, round and wide-open. The noses should be shortish, but not as flat as those of the Long-hairs. To prevent loss of type, that is the noses becoming too long or the ears too tall, it has been found necessarily to out-cross occasionally with a Long-hair. This should not be done too frequently, as there is the danger of the coat becoming fluffy, rather than close and fine. The Manx is included with the British cats, but is, of course, unique in its taillessness, and there are slight differences in type and coat.

In the States Domestic Short-hairs have the same colours and coat patterns as in Britain, but the heads are not quite so broad. There are also cats very like the Britishers, but the heads are even rounder and the ears smaller. These are known as the Exotics.

Possibly, because of their ancestry, British Short-hairs have a good reputation for catching mice and rats. They make wonderful pets, having calm natures and taking anything in their stride. They love lots of attention and show affection readily.

Condition is important, and for a cat to look a picture of health the eyes should be bright and shining, with no dirt in the corners, and the ears should be quite clean inside. Even with the short fur, a certain amount of grooming is desirable. Too much combing tends to make the fur look too open, so brushing or hard hand stroking is better. This will get rid of the old hairs in the coat. If your cat is a hunter, particular watch should be kept for the occasional flea. I live in the country, and have known my cats to return from rabbit hunting with the edges of their ears lined with small fleas. They also pick them up from hedgehog runs, but a little suitable insecticide, sprinkled in the fur and combed out with a tooth comb, should soon get rid of the pests.

Short-haired   WHITE

Short-haired Whites, with their almost translucent coats, are extremely popular. As in the Long-hairs, there are the two varieties, one with blue eyes and the other with orange, with the odd eyes appearing occasionally. It is just as difficult in the Short-hairs to produce cats with bright blue eye colour; the blue is often far too pale. The difficulty is to find suitable studs to improve the eyes. Here again many of the cats with blue eyes are deaf. Certain strains are not affected, and kittens born with a black smudge on the forehead, like a thumb-mark, frequently have good hearing, even if the black hairs go as the kitten coat grows out. This deafness is thought to be connected with albinism—although a true albino is pink-eyed, and I have never seen this in a white cat. Whites with orange eyes are easier to breed, possibly because the one or two Long-hairs used to improve the type re-introduce good orange eye colour.

Short coats are easier to keep in order, even if white. Talcum powder may be sprinkled thoroughly into the roots and then brushed out to remove any grease or dirt. Whites can be bathed in the sink with warm water. Make a lather with a suitable shampoo (those recommended for poodles are ideal). This should be rubbed thoroughly into the coat, care being taken to avoid the eyes and ears. The fur should be rinsed several times. If the cat doesn't object, drying with a hair dryer is most effective. When dry, hard hand stroking will restore some of the natural grease to the coat.

68

44 Odd-eyed Whit

46 'We are not amused'

Whites turn up in litters from Tortoiseshells and Tortoiseshell-and-Whites may even appear in litters from black cats, and, of course, from pure white breeding. There have been some wonderful specimens at the Shows in recent years, but unfortunately they are very rare.

The charming stair-climbing cat in figure 44 is a typical example of odd eyes: the difference in the colour of the two eyes can be clearly seen. Lucinda and Lucifer belonging to Mrs Pearson (46) are lovely examples of the orange-eyed variety.

71

Short-haired BLACK

As there are so many short-coated black cats around, people are often surprised to learn that there is a Short-haired pedigree variety. It is not until one has seen a really splendid champion Black that the difference between pet and pedigree is appreciated. Bimbo has beautiful eyes and well-rounded ears (47).

The pedigree cats should have a shining jet black coat, with no white hairs anywhere, the type being as for the other Britishers, and whereas the pet cats invariably have green eyes, those of the pedigree should be deep copper or orange with no trace of green. Damp and hot sunshine may cause brown tinges on the coat.

Frequently Blacks appear as the result of Siamese mis-matings, but these are invariably foreign in type, with almond-shaped eyes, although the fur may be a splendid black.

It is strange that the black cats portrayed as bringers of good luck invariably have British type, with broad cheerful faces, while those connected with black magic, shown flying with witches on their brooms, have long slinky bodies and slits for eyes. Harrison Weir, writing on black cats only 80 years ago says: 'the black cat is held by the prejudiced ignorant as an animal most foul and detestable, and wonderful stories are related of their actions in the dead of night during thunderstorms and windy nights'. Alas, superstition dies hard, and it is not so very long ago that black cats were suspected of being the devil's familiars, and in both Europe and the United States were often hung, tortured or burned along with their innocent owners, who were suspected of being witches.

Not that this is the reason for the small numbers of Blacks today. No, I think there are so few, as would-be breeders feel there would be little demand for kittens, and prefer to go in for, what they feel, are more popular varieties.

A Black may be used as a mate for Tortoiseshells and Tortoiseshell-and-Whites, and is also now being used to produce the recently re-recognised Bi-Colours.

73

47 *Mrs Jeffery's Bimbo*

48 *British Blue crossbred with a White*

Short-haired BRITISH BLUE

The most popular of the Short-haired British varieties, and probably the one which comes closest to the set standard, as may be seen by the photograph of Champion Pensylva Mirus (49). He has a typical round head, with chubby cheeks, rounded ears, and big round eyes.

British Blues are usually muscular big sturdy cats, and particularly when neutered, having no urge to wander, make excellent pets, as they love affection. The colour may be a light to medium blue, but must be the same all over, with no shadings, white hairs or markings in the coat. The fur texture is important. It should never be harsh to the touch, but short and soft.

The classes at the Shows are very well filled, and any kittens offered for sale there usually go very quickly. In fact, often there is a waiting list for the kittens, a clear indication of their popularity.

The little kitten in figure 48 is probably the result of cross-breeding with a White. He certainly has blue in him, but would have to be shown in the

74

49 *Ch. Pensylva Miru*

50 *Pensylva
Jane with litter*

'Any Other Variety' class, not the 'British Blue'. His eyes are in the process of changing from blue to orange.

Like the Long-haired Blues, by cross-matings with Creams or Blue Creams, they may be used to produce a varied litter (see Blue Cream Long-hairs in figure 18). Pensylva Jane (50) is a Blue Cream, but has both Blues and Creams in her litter. The shadow markings often seen on young self-coloured kittens, even the Long-haired ones, may be seen quite clearly in the photograph, but these vanish with the growth of the fur.

This close-up of a British Blue shows clearly the large round eyes and the shape of the pupils. Cats cannot see in complete darkness but can see better than humans in a very dim light. Their pupils contract to a mere slip in bright sunshine and open wide in the dark. This enables them to hunt at night. Cats' eyes shine out in the dark because they reflect light.

The nicitating membrane, or the third eyelid, forms a protection to their eyes. In the event of illness or poor condition due to worms, it may partly cover the corner of the eye: this condition is referred to as 'the haw being up'.

51 'Cat's Eyes'

HAVING KITTENS

This unique picture (52) shows a kitten only just born. Whilst the mother is attending to the next addition, her owner is assisting by wiping the first arrival dry. It will then be tucked up beside the mother for her to finish the job and to keep it warm.

To start from the beginning, gestation—the time which elapses between mating and the birth of the kittens—may be anything from 63–65 days, and sometimes a day or two over this. Owners should not panic if their cat's kittens are overdue, as long as she seems fit and well, and is eating her food.

A box should be ready in a darkened corner, well away from any interference. This box should be long enough for the cat to stretch out in. I always use a cardboard one, which can be thrown away when no longer needed, but there are some really splendid specially made maternity boxes. I have seen one which was ideal; this measured about 18 by 20 inches and was about 15 inches high and was made from painted plywood. The top was hinged as a lid, so that the owner could open it and look in without disturbing the proceedings unless absolutely necessary. Across the front was a bar of wood, about 4 inches high, to prevent the kittens from rolling out. The whole of the front was covered with washable curtains, which could be easily pushed on one side when the kittens were old enough to scramble in and out. Another one was constructed on the same principle, with a hinged top, but instead of curtains in front the box was solid, with a large circle taken out to enable the mother to clamber in and out at will.

For the birth itself I feel clean newspaper is best in the boxes. Some cats, many days before the kittens are due, spend their time preparing a nest, tearing the paper into strips with their teeth, so I always provide quite a thick wad for this. I even had one cat who pulled out some of her fur and pushed this in among the shredded paper. Since having kittens is a perfectly natural process for the cat, leave her to cope on her own, unless she seems to be straining for a long time without results, and is obviously in pain. Usually a cat will bite through the cord and wash the kittens without any assistance. It is as well to have a warm hot bottle covered with a blanket in another box, so that if there is a rush of kittens and the mother seems worried about the first-born, they can nestle quietly on the hot water bottle until all the kittens have arrived. They must be kept warm, and not allowed to get

78

chilled. When all is over, remove the soiled newspaper, and replace with a thick warm blanket that will not ruck up and cover any of the kittens. She will probably be grateful for a warm drink of milk or baby food with a little glucose added, and should settle down to sleep. The kittens will probably start suckling at once.

A nursing mother should be given an extra meal a day to keep her in good condition, and to ensure the kittens are strong and healthy. Weaning of the kittens may start when they are three weeks old, by giving a drop or two of the baby milk, gradually increasing up to one teaspoonful. Weaning should be spread over 5–6 weeks, with first one meal a day of Lactol or baby milk, made according to the directions on the tin, followed by the introduction of a second meal the next week. A little solid food may be given when the kittens are about 4–5 weeks old. This could be cooked white fish or a little scraped raw meat. It is important never to rush the weaning, and to introduce any new item just a little at a time. As some kittens are more greedy than others, it is better to give each one a separate dish.

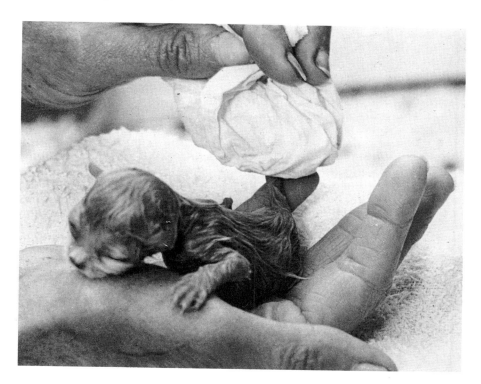

Two minutes old

53   *Ch. Pensylva Prince D'or*

Short-haired   CREAM

This is a variety that has made great strides during recent years. It used to be said the coat colouring was too red, but now, as may be seen from the outstanding colour photograph of the Pensylva mother with her kitten (54), Creams can be bred with fur of a rich even cream. There is still a tendency for the tails to have shadow rings.

Creams may appear in litters from Tortoiseshells and Tortoiseshell-and-Whites, but are more often the result of Blue Cream breeding. The type is usually very good. The eyes may be copper or hazel in colour. Thirty-five points are allowed for the coat colour alone, 15 for the eyes, and the remaining 50, which is the same for all Short-hairs, for type, coat and condition.

Condition is very important in a cat, and yet it is difficult to define. A cat in good condition will look alert and healthy, the eyes will be bright and shining, and the ears held at the correct angle to the head. Even the fur will look springy and full of life, and the tail will be held up. A cat in poor condition would certainly lose marks at a Show, as the fur would look spikey and the eyes dull. It may be possible to feel its spine if a hand is run along the back, and the tail may be between the back legs. This condition can be caused by worms, incorrect feeding, or a serious illness.

Some owners feed incorrectly through sheer ignorance, thinking anything will do. Very few people nowadays have enough scraps left over to feed their cat. An adult cat needs two good meals a day. Raw meat with a few corn-flakes or brown bread added, cooked rabbit or any cooked meat, heart, a little cooked liver, cooked white fish with the bones removed, tinned pilchards, are all good items to include in the diet. The fat should be left on the meat (provided it is not excessive) and not cut off, as some is necessary for the cat's well-being. Green vegetables may be given if liked. Milk is not an essential; in fact it cannot be tolerated by some cats, particularly Siamese, and may cause them diarrhoea. But all my Long-hairs drink it by the saucerful with no trouble. It is particularly important that clean drinking water should always be available. Tinned cat foods are very good as a stand-by, or as a part of the diet, but few firms producing them claim that they are sufficient by themselves. Grass too should be grown in a pot for the cat to chew, if there is no garden.

81

55   *Pensylva Cream kitten*

55   *Pensylva Cream kitten*

55   *Pensylva Cream kitten*

54   *Mrs Richard's Short-haired Creams*

Short-haired BLUE CREAM

It is very difficult to breed a short-haired Blue Cream with the hairs inter-mingled, rather than patched. It is more easily accomplished in the Long-hairs, but some of the Short-hairs look more like Tortoiseshells with solid patches of blue and cream. These are considered excellent in the States, where the standard says that the short fur should be blue with patches of solid cream. Blue Creams are an all-female variety, and when mated to British Blues or Creams, could produce Creams, Blues, and Blue Creams—hence Penysylva Jane's mixed litter (50). They make excellent mothers, seeming to enjoy the amusing antics of their varied-coloured kittens.

56 Blue Cream and Cream kitten

Many owners of female kittens ring me up for advice on the subject of neutering, or spaying, as it is called when a female cat is involved. If the owner has no intention of letting the cat have kittens, spaying is the answer. It is possible for a cat to have a litter, and be spayed afterwards. A female kitten can come into season or 'call' at a very early age—five months not being unknown for some varieties. This is far too young to start having kittens, and she should be carefully guarded, away from all male cats. It depends on a kitten's development, but 4–5 months is probably the best age for spaying. It is more serious than the neutering of a male kitten, necessitating a small cut in the side and one or two stitches. If kept quiet for a day or two, on a light diet, the kitten will soon recover. Once the stitches are removed the fur will grow rapidly and soon cover the scar. A neutered female still makes a delightful pet, and with sufficient exercise should not grow fat. Moreover the owner will not be plagued by calling male cats, as would happen if the female were allowed to call time and time again without mating.

Short-haired   BI-COLOURED

This is a newly recognised variety, still very rare. In fact, it's probably impossible to breed a cat with the precise divisions of colour given in the standard: 'The self colour, that is Black, Blue, Orange or Cream (the possible colour variations allowed) to start immediately behind the shoulders, round the legs, leaving the hind feet white. White shoulders, neck, forelegs and feet, chin, lips and blaze up face and over the top of head, joining or running into the white at back of skull, thus dividing the mask exactly in half. The markings to follow those of a Dutch-marked rabbit as closely as possible. The eyes may be copper or amber, with the type as for the other British Short-hairs.'

Of course, there are a number of very attractive Short-haired cats with two-coloured coats. The little blue and white Pathfinder kitten (58) would fall in this category, but would fall short of the standard. Bi-Colours are most useful in producing Tortoiseshells and Tortoiseshell-and-Whites.

Many would-be owners are worried at the thought of their new pets scratching the furniture, doing what is frequently referred to as 'sharpening the claws'. Most cats and kittens need something to scratch on, but not so much to sharpen the claws, as to keep them clean and to rub down the worn part. If a cat's claws become too long, a vet should clip them for you, as unless this is done correctly, too much may be cut off, causing bleeding of the quick.

Kittens must be trained from an early age not to scratch on the furniture. I have found it most effective to point a finger and say 'No' sharply. If there is a garden with trees or wooden posts, the kitten should be trained to scratch on these. If no garden, scratching posts sold by pet shops are quite effective. A piece of old carpet nailed to a board, string wrapped around the table leg, or a log of wood may all be used, but the kitten must be shown how to use them. De-clawing, that is removing the whole claws, is a major operation, and is banned by the Governing Council of the Cat Fancy. Any de-clawed cat or kitten would be refused entry to a Show.

Short-haired   SPOTTED

These are the latest thing in cats, and they are now appearing at the Shows in ever increasing numbers. This is strange, because the 'Spotties' are the oldest

86

58 *Pathfinder Bi-Colour*

domestic cats known, with similar markings being seen on many of the smaller wild cats. At the beginning of the century there were quite a number, and they would appear at Shows penned side by side with the occasional small wild felines, such as the margay. Then, no one seems to know why, the pedigree ones appeared to die out, and up to recent years the spotting had only been seen on one or two pet cats.

On various wild cats the coats may be covered with spots in different shapes, some large and round, others smaller, some oblong and others rosette. In the pedigree variety, the spots too may be any shape, but they must be clear and distinct, not merging into one another. The whole body should be spotted, even the tummy, and a fine example of this may be seen in the picture of the two little kittens trying to attract attention at the Cat Show (60). Any background colour is permitted, as long as the spots form a distinct contrast. Culverden Stardust (59) is an excellent example of a bright silver with contrasting black spots. She was bred by Miss I. Robson and is owned by Mrs E. Menezes. I have also seen a very good Red with darker red spots, and there are many other possible colour variations.

89

61 Silver Tabby kitten

Short-haired TABBIES

The same pattern of markings is required for the Tabbies with short coats as for the Long-haired, but naturally the pattern is more striking in the short fur, and the markings more definite.

There are also short-haired Tabbies with mackerel markings—the markings being rings rather than forming a pattern. Their standard says that the rings should be as narrow as possible and as numerous, running vertically from the spine towards the ground. These may have the same colour variations as the patterned Tabbies, but those I have seen recently have had silver background fur with black rings. Tabbies may be brown, silver and red.

90

62 Short-haired Silver Tabby

The 'M' mark required in the standard shows up very clearly on the head of the Sleeping Beauty in figure 61, while the lovely creature facing her (62) has most definite 'Lord Mayor's chains', and really gorgeous eyes.

Short-haired   SILVER TABBY

Champion Hillcross Silver Petal, bred by Mrs Towe and owned by Miss I. Robson, shows a fine pattern of markings, and has a good round head, with big round eyes. Culverden Clair de Lune's litter (64) contains both striped and mackerel kittens, and she is evidently a very proud mother, allowing nothing to interfere with the job in hand.

The Silver Tabby is rapidly increasing in popularity, running the British Blues very close, and the kittens find ready buyers. Sturdy, independent cats, my own Silver Tabbies had a very aristocratic background, but were still wonderful at catching rats and mice.

It should be realised that, even if kept on a farm or in the country where

92

rats and mice are around for the catching, no cat should be expected to live on vermin alone and needs feeding as well. Those that go out rabbiting may pick up a few fleas, and if any scratching is noticed, the coat should be gone through with a small tooth comb to remove these. It may be necessary to use an insecticide powder on the coat, but this should all be brushed out after about five minutes. The animal should not be allowed to lick the fur while the powder is in it, and the insecticide used must be one recommended as suitable for cats and kittens, and not contain DDT. In any case, no such powder should be used on very young kittens. Constant careful combing should deal with their fleas effectively.

Short-haired   RED TABBY

The coat should be a rich red and the markings a darker rich red, the pattern standing out distinctly from the background. There is no connection between these aristocratic beauties and the ubiquitous ginger toms, who are usually sandy or pale marmalade.

    One of the earliest writers on cats, Gordon Stables, says of the Red Tabbies

95

5   Red Tabby kitten

in *The Domestic Cat* (1876): 'They are the prettiest of pets, and the honestest of all cat kind. They are such good ratters that neither mice nor rats will frequent the house they inhabit.'

They are great favourites as pets, particularly with men. As most are neutered, they grow into massive tough-looking animals, but their appearance belies them, as they are usually as gentle as the kitten in figure 66. Note that his eyes are still changing colour, and his markings are not yet clearly defined. The little Reds in figure 65 are a lovely red, but as the one at the back has a very white chin, I feel sure their mother was a Tortie-and-White.

Tabby cats in Norfolk and Suffolk were once referred to as 'Cyprus' cats. Some dictionaries give one definition of the word 'cyprus' as tabby, while another says that it is a reddish-yellow colour. So the early Cyprus cats were probably Red or Orange Tabbies. The actual word 'tabby' is said to have come from Baghdad, from the Attabiya district, where a watered silk was made. The markings on a Tabby cat were thought to resemble those on the silk, but I feel it may have been the other way round.

Short-haired   BROWN TABBY

Brown Tabbies often appear among pet cats, and probably because of this there are few people interested in breeding the pedigree variety, although the the pets seldom have the rich sable brown fur colour required in the standard. Admittedly some pets have very good markings, and, in fact, I have owned one myself. The one opposite (67) has a wonderful head but his markings are mackerel. The type is typically British, with full cheeks, big round eyes, and rounded ears. Brown Tabbies make excellent family pets, full of fun and vigour, yet seldom aggressive.

A male house pet should be neutered before he develops the unpleasant habit of spraying, so that the whole place smells of 'tom-cat'. Neutering is only a minor operation if carried out at about $3\frac{1}{2}$ months. If not neutered, most males will roam the neighbourhood looking for likely female cats, becoming involved with other male cats en route and returning with battle scars. If there is a female cat in season around, he will probably stay out all night. If possible all cats should be kept in at night, as so many get killed

96

or seriously injured by cars. The little charmer in figure 68 is a typical Brown Tabby. He is sure to be up to every imaginable mischief, and care must be taken to see that he does not stray on to the road.

69 *Tortoiseshell kitten in a mixed litter*

Short-haired TORTOISESHELL

The demure little lady in the basket (69) shows the bright colours required in the Tortoiseshells, i.e. black, red and cream. Her brother and sister illustrate well the mixed litter that may be born to a Tortie. I think all their whiskers are simply splendid.

99

68 *Brown Tabby kitten*

The remarks on the possibilities of breeding Long-haired kittens of this variety (see page 33) also apply to those with short coats. This too being an all-female variety, a male of one of the self-colours is the best choice for a mate.

The Tortoiseshell bred by Miss Woodifield (70) shows up very well the tiny coloured patches on the ears and the 'broken' paws. A red blaze on the face is liked.

Tortoiseshells are a very old variety, and have been featured in paintings by the Masters over the centuries. They were so called because it was thought that the mottling of the fur resembled the shells of the tortoises.

They have a reputation for being good mothers, but teach their kittens independence at an early age, leaving them to play among themselves while they go off hunting—sometimes to return with a dead rabbit or mouse, which is proudly presented to the babies.

70 *Pathfinder Tortoiseshell*

Short-haired TORTOISESHELL-AND-WHITE

The sturdy matron opposite with brightly patched coat is a typical Tortoiseshell-and-White. All her legs have some patches of colour which is good, but she would probably be penalised by the judge for the white hairs appearing in the dark patches. It is very seldom that one finds a cat with entirely distinct patching, inevitably there is some smudging of the colours. Any stripes on the coat would be considered a very bad fault. This is another all-female variety, making it hard to find suitable males to produce kittens like the mother.

The little kitten prepared to hold her own against all comers (73) shows well the colours of this variety, but here again the patches are spoiled by brindling. Not that this matters when choosing a pet; it would only be faulted on the show bench. The Tortie-and-White in figure 72 has a very nice expression and lovely eyes, but there is very little black on her head and her coat is rather too long. All the same she is a beauty, and I know there will be many who would like to own her.

72 *Long-haired Tortoiseshell*

73 *Tortie-and-White*

74 *Brightwell–Manx kitten*

Short-haired   MANX

Unique in its taillessness, the Manx is the subject of many legends, ranging from the first Manx landing on the Isle of Man after the wreck of the Spanish Armada to the cat's tail having been cut off by Noah slamming the door when it only just managed to get inside before the sailing of the Ark.

It is included in the British section, but apart from the taillessness there are also other differences. The coat should be 'double', soft and open on top, like that of a rabbit, with soft thick undercoat. The head is large and round, but the nose is longish, and the cheeks very prominent. The ears should be rather wide at the base, tapering slightly off to a point, rather than rounded. The back should be short, with the rump entirely round, like an orange, with not the slightest suspicion of a tail. In fact, it should be possible to place the top of one's thumb in the hollow where the tail should start. Due to the height of the hindquarters and the depth of the flanks, Manx have a walk all of their own, referred to as 'a rabbit-like gait'.

104

In order that the breed should not die out, the Isle of Man has established a cattery on the island, and there are also a number of breeders in this country. Some excellent specimens appear at the Shows, but it is not always possible to produce Manx to order. Continually breeding Manx to Manx produces a lethal factor, with the kittens dying prior to or just after birth. Litters may contain kittens with tails, some with stumps and perhaps some Manx.

The coat and eye colour is immaterial. The splendid white specimen below (75) illustrates well the rounded rump and high hindquarters, with the little tabby and white kitten bred by Mrs K. Butcher (74) having all the makings of a future champion.

The lack of tail seems to make no difference to a Manx's activities, as they climb, leap and jump about just like other cats.

75 An All-white Manx

Short-haired   ANY OTHER VARIETY

This has been given a breed number so that cats unlike any other variety may be registered, and then, if the owner wishes, they may be shown in the pedigree section of a Show. They cannot compete for challenge certificates, and while registered as 'Any Other Variety' cannot be Champions.

Cats registered under this category may be the result of cross-matings;

have unusual colouring; or may be a new variety, not yet given a standard, making its bow to the public for the first time.

The blue and white Short-haired cat displaying her musical talent opposite (76) belongs to no particular variety, but her markings look almost like a saddle on her back, and, who knows, someone may be trying to produce cats with these particular markings.

The black and white in figure 77 may have been produced from a Short- and Long-haired cross. She is a most attractive cat, much loved by her owner, who happens to be the same age as the cat, 14 years.

Foreign Short-haired cats

Both the British and Foreign varieties are Short-haired cats, but there the similarity ends, as what is considered a good point in one variety is often a bad one in the other. Whereas the Britisher is a 'square' with round head and short body, the Foreigns (and this includes the Siamese as well) have long slim bodies on slim legs, and wedge-shaped heads. The ears are sharp, comparatively large, and broad at the base. The tails are long and tapering, and the eyes almond-shaped, referred to as 'oriental'. Each variety differs slightly from the others. They should be cats of medium size, with short close coats.

They differ in character, as well as looks from the British Short-hairs. Though all affectionate and home-loving, they are markedly independent.

The majority of the Foreign Short-hairs have been developed in Britain and few can claim genuine ancestry with the cats of the country after which they have been named. Maybe, in the first place, one or two may have been imported from the country after which they are named, but the truth is that inter-breeding, cross-breeding and out-breeding is responsible for the many delightful varieties we have today. Even today one or two fanciers have worked hard on a specialised breeding programme and have succeeded in producing two new varieties—the Foreign White and the Self Lilac. Neither of these has yet been recognised, but I expect they, and many others yet to be produced, will receive breed numbers in the years to come. In the States there is now a hairless cat, and one referred to as 'wire-haired'. (Hairless cats were, however, known in Mexico at the beginning of the century, so perhaps they can scarcely be termed as a new variety.) For the first time Short-hairs now outnumber Long-hairs in the States. Surprisingly, this increase is not entirely caused by the continuing popularity of the Siamese, but is also due to many more breeders becoming interested in Abyssinians and Brown Burmese.

As well as endeavouring to produce new varieties, fanciers try to breed out any characteristics not approved of, such as badly kinked tails, and the crossed eyes of some Siamese. A very slight kink at the extreme tip of the tail is permitted in some breeds, but a very bad one is now frowned on, and in the case of a Long-hair this may mean disqualification.

Some cat-fanciers love Long-hairs and abhor Siamese, whilst others say the Long-hairs are dull in comparison to the very lively Burmese. Well, it takes all sorts. . . . Despite the saying that at night all cats are grey, by daylight every one is entirely different, and like humans, they all have their own personalities, likes and dislikes.

ABYSSINIAN

The colouring of Abyssinian cats is very like that of the caffre cats, from which it is said the first domestic cats are descended. They are also said to closely resemble the cats worshipped in Ancient Egypt; certainly their outline is similar to those seen in Egyptian wall paintings and statuettes. Abyssinian cats were first seen in England in 1869, and were supposed to have been brought from Abyssinia. Although this is possible, there appear to be few or no cats answering their description in that country today. But, whatever their origin, and however much people argue about it, they are cats of great charm, with wonderful personalities.

The colour of the 'Standard' Abyssinian is a ruddy brown, with each hair of the coat being banded with two or three rings of black or dark brown. Though the type is foreign, it should never be too extreme, and the ears should not be as large as those of the Siamese. The pads of the feet are black, with the colour extending up the back of the hind legs. The large expressive eyes may be green, yellow or hazel. The chins should be cream, but are very often white, which is a fault, but is most difficult to breed out. A white locket or white spot on the underside is looked on as a definite blemish.

The tickings can be seen distinctly in the black and white photograph (80) of Contented Tonga, owned by Mrs Menezes. He is a good example of this variety, with no bars or markings, and has beautiful tufted ears. The kittens in figures 78–9 are definitely cross-bred and would certainly lose marks for their tabby markings, when being judged. The twin kittens in figure 82 are very sweet, and their 'Lord Mayor's chains' around their necks may become less distinct when the adult stage is reached.

Abyssinians rarely have litters of more than four in number, and for some reason, more males are born than females, which is a pity, for there is always a demand for the females for breeding. Some of our best Abyssinians have been exported all over the world, including California, Australia, New Zealand—and even Abyssinia!

80   Mrs Menezes' Contented Tong

RED ABYSSINIAN

From time to time over the years since Abyssinians were first recognised, a kitten would be born in a litter that differed in colour from its brothers and sisters. Although no doubts could be expressed as to the mother's virtue—strict precautions would have been taken, and all the kittens were obviously by the same sire—the kitten with a red coat differed from the standard and had, therefore, to be registered as 'Any Other Variety'. Breeders complained about this, and as more kittens with red coats appeared from certain strains, they were eventually granted a breed number, were recognised as a separate variety, and were thus able to compete for Championships.

Where this Red strain comes from no one knows, but they are certainly most attractive. In the United States they are called 'Sorrel', which is a very good description of their colour. The British standard says that the body colour should be a rich copper red, the hairs being double or treble ticked with

114

82   *Twin Abyssinian kitte*

an even darker red. The pads are pink, not black as those with the ruddy brown coats.

Ch. Philos Precious Tapos owned by Miss H. Scatchard (81) is a wonderful example of the Red Abyssinian. His coat is beautifully ticked, and, although in black and white his chin and under the neck looks white, the colour is really cream, which is permissible.

Some grooming is necessary to keep them looking really beautiful. Hard stroking with the hand or with a brush with hair bristles should remove all the old hairs, and some breeders find that a few drops of bay rum, sprinkled well into the fur and then brushed out, gives it just a slight gloss.

Whether a standard Abyssinian or one with a Red coat, either makes a wonderful pet. The kittens are very forward, climbing out of their basket when only a week or two old. They can be taught when old enough to sit up and beg, like a dog, and will wave their paws around, asking for tit-bits.

BROWN BURMESE

Britain can claim credit for having introduced practically all the varieties of pedigree cats to the rest of the world, and is, therefore, responsible for the whole Cat Fancy today, with an ever-increasing flow of pedigree stock being exported. The sole exception is the Burmese.

In 1930 Dr J. Thompson took a Brown Burmese, named Wong Mau, from India to the United States, and she was the first ever seen there. Eventually pure-bred Burmese were produced, and it was from the States in 1947 that they became the first new breed to be exported from that country to Britain. They are now doing so well that they are second to the Siamese in popularity.

They are not Brown Siamese, as I have heard it said, but differ on many points. The body should not be so long, and the wedge-shaped head shorter, the top of the head being slightly rounded. The ears should be relatively large, wide at the base and slightly rounded at the tip. The large lustrous eyes should be clear golden yellow, never green. It is proving rather difficult to get quite the correct eye colour preferred, and at the moment, they have eyes of chartreuse yellow.

Grooming of Short-hairs is just as important as that of the Long-hairs, although not quite so arduous. The ears need the same attention, a gentle

116

wipe with cotton wool to remove any dust, and attention by the vet should there be any signs of a discharge. The corners of the eyes should be free of any dirt. If in good condition the coat has a beautiful sheen, and hard hand stroking or the use of short bristled brush should remove all the old hairs, and give the short fine fur an even more glossy look.

Brown Burmese kittens are lighter in colour than the mother when born, almost coffee colour in fact, and it is possible that faint contrasting points and mask may be seen for the first few months, but these should fade. If these do persist into adulthood, they would be considered a fault. There should be no white or tabby markings, although a few white hairs should not penalise an otherwise outstanding cat.

The Brown Burmese, owned by Mrs A. Sayer (83), is shown in a typical

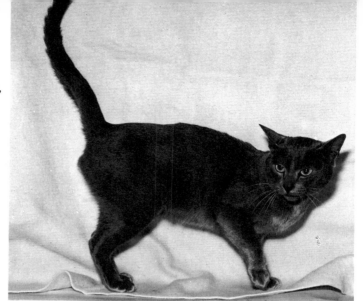

85 *Ch. Freefolk Blue Buoy,*
Blue Burmese

Burmese stance, showing interest in anything the slightest bit unusual that is going on. The little kitten in the colour photograph (84) shows the lighter coat of kittenhood. His chest is not really cream, but is the reflection of the light on the fur.

BLUE BURMESE

After its importation from America in 1947, the Brown Burmese reigned supreme in Britain for several years. It was then discovered that from certain strains Burmese with blue coats were appearing. In all characteristics they were identical to the Brown, but the fur in the adult cats was a bluish grey, darker on the back, and shading to pale fawn or grey on the underside, the whole coat having a distinctive silver sheen. When young, the kittens were more fawn than blue. This colour was much admired, and now there are very many Blue Burmese about. They are not yet recognised in America.

The Burmese should never be a fat cat, but should not be too lean either. A good specimen should give the impression of a strong muscular cat. The eyes are almond-shaped, slanting towards the nose, and should be a yellowish-green to yellow in colour.

As there is a certain amount of controversy regarding the correct eye colour of the Burmese, I think I should quote a footnote from the Official standard: 'Because of their low colour intensity, the apparent colour of

119

84 *Brown Burmese kitten*

86 *Blue and Brown Burmese, owned by Mrs Gray*

Burmese eyes is greatly affected by the colour and intensity of the light in which they are viewed. They should be judged in moderately strong diffused daylight.' Judges of the Burmese are given a piece of yellow silk ribbon so that they may have a clearer indication of the actual colour required.

They make delightful pets, and if their training is started when young they will take readily to a lead. They usually travel well, and one I know accompanies his mistress everywhere, sitting looking out of the car window so as not to miss a minute of the journey.

CHESTNUT BROWN FOREIGN

These are known as Havanas in the United States. They are an example of a man-made breed, which took many years of selective breeding, and the discarding of a number of kittens not quite up to the colour standard as pets, before it became possible to produce a cat with three generations of pure colour breeding behind it. The Governing Council of the Cat Fancy will never consider giving a breed number, that is recognising a standard, until evidence of pure breeding is supplied, and also proof that there are enough fanciers interested in the new variety.

The Chestnut Brown is most attractive, self-coloured, without shadow points as may occasionally be seen in the Burmese. The colour should be that of red-brown glossy chestnuts, the coat being fine and short. It is a fine-boned animal, of foreign type, and should never be too heavy. The oriental-shaped eyes should be a decided green. The tail long and whiplike, and even the whiskers should be brown. Any white hairs in the coat would be considered a fault.

They are still comparatively rare, but quite a number of these elegant cats have been exported to various parts of the world.

87   Mrs Dunnill's Chestnut Brown

89 *Annelida*
Rex at nine weeks

CORNISH AND DEVON REX

Throughout the centuries, as far as is known, cats were always born with straight hair, either long or short in length. But in 1950 on a farm in Cornwall, a kitten with a curly coat was born in a litter from farm cats. Fortunately, the owner realised this was unique, and in an endeavour to produce others with similar coats eventually mated the little male back to his Tortoiseshell-and-White mother; this resulted in more curly-coated kittens. The curly coat

123

was already known in rabbits, and these had been called Rex, so the same name was given to these kittens.

A number of cat fanciers, naturally interested in anything new in the cat world, realised that this was a mutation, relating entirely to the hairs of the fur, and was not a new variety. They appreciated the possibilities of producing the curly coats in cats of all colours.

In 1960 a curly-coated kitten appeared in a litter in Devon, and, as it was the next-door county to Cornwall, it was presumed that there must be some connection between the two. Cross-matings were tried, without success, straight-haired kittens only resulting, and it was realised that the Devon and the Cornish were caused by two different genes. Strangely enough about this time, curly-coated kittens were also born in the United States, and in Germany. The curly-coated kittens caught the public fancy, and many were exported to all parts of the world.

In due course both the Devon and the Rex received recognition. The standards are very similar, saying that the two types should have long and slender bodies of medium size and long fine tails; but whereas the head of the Cornish should have a straight profile, that of the Devon should have a nose with a definite stop. The coats should be dense, short and fine, but I have found that the Cornish usually has a slightly thicker wavy coat than that of the Devon.

Any coat colour or pattern is permitted, and the curliness has been introduced into both the Burmese and the Siamese. The Sicat bred by Mrs Lidyard playing on the trolley (92) is an excellent example of this. He still has the distinctive coat pattern of the Siamese, but his coat is definitely wavy.

The Annelida Rex kitten bred by Mrs Ashford (89) is intrigued by his own reflection, and also is showing up the waves on his tummy, while Curley Koon, the black Cornish Rex (88) looks as if he has come straight from the hairdresser, so perfect are the waves and curls on his coat. Even the whiskers are curly.

Kismet, a Rex bred by Mrs Ashford, has a wonderful shaped head, and also feels that all this photography business is enough to make a cat laugh. Note in particular his tongue (91).

Cats' tongues are unusual. They are covered with tiny hooks referred to as papillae. It is the roughness caused by the papillaea that enables cats to lick

124

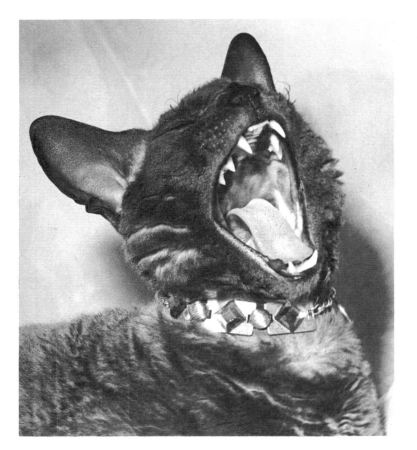

plates clean, to lap up milk and water, and of course, to wash themselves
thoroughly.

    I should like to say a little about taking cats in cars. They should not be
allowed to wander freely, as some sudden noise may make them jump onto
their owner's lap, possibly causing an accident. If they do not like being on a
lead, it is better to use a basket with an open-wire mesh end, so that they can
see out, but cannot get in the way of the brake, or get stuck under the seat.
Not all cats like car travel. Some sit and dribble all the time, and unless the
travel is essential, these would be much happier at home. If they have to travel,
and become panic-stricken, a vet will prescribe a tranquilliser. This should

126

never be given prior to a Show, as there may be a violent reaction when the effect of the drug wears off. It is for this reason that the Governing Council of the Cat Fancy inserts a notice in all Show schedules that a cat found to be suffering from drugs is subject to expulsion from the Show on the authority of the vet.

92   Sicat, bred by Mrs Lidyard

RUSSIAN BLUE

In the nineteenth century sailors are said to have brought Short-haired blue-coated cats from Archangel to Britain. There are, moreover, old tales in Russia which mention little blue cats. At the time there were already various Short-haired blue-coated cats in Britain, some home bred, some from Malta, others from Spain and yet others from America. Eventually there were two classes at the early Cat Shows, with a separate one for those with Foreign type. In the end the name 'Russian' was decided on for those with the short, silky coats, long bodies and long heads. Unfortunately, in the meantime, in an effort to improve the type, cross-breeding with Siamese and other varieties had been tried, but by so doing often the wonderful silvery sheen of the coat was lost, and shadow rings were introduced to the tail, and many fanciers lost interest in the Russians. Challenge certificates were frequently withheld, and the breed was threatened with extinction. To combat this, several dedicated fanciers banded together and, keeping to a strict programme, have now managed to produce Russian Blues of pure breeding.

The standard says that the Russian Blue should be lithe, long and snaky, fine in bone, with a decidedly longish face and narrowish skull, with rather large and pointed ears. The point that distinguishes it from all other cats, whether Blue or not, is the fur, which should be short, close and lustrous, with a sealskin-like texture. The ears too are a distinctive feature. They should be large and pointed, with the skin being thin and transparent, with very little inside furnishing.

They have wonderful characters, and have a reputation for being exceptionally quiet cats. In fact, it is sometimes not easy to tell when the females are in season. They are dainty creatures, on long slim legs, with small oval feet.

Ch. Hengist Stroganoff bred by Mrs N. Fiske (93) has a typical stud face, hence the heavy jowls. Note too the prominent whisker pads, which are a feature of this particular variety.

FOREIGN WHITE

The attractive little White below (94) belongs to Mrs M. Dunnill, and is an example of the Foreign Whites. This man-made variety has a proposed standard, but cannot yet compete in a breed class of its own.

They are self-coloured Whites with foreign type, fine boned and, as can be seen, are very graceful cats. At the moment, the oriental-shaped eyes may be golden yellow or bright blue. This is a created breed, which means that many years have had to be spent to find the right cats to use to produce the correct outline without losing the pure white coat.

94   Mrs Dunnill's Foreign White kitten

FOREIGN LILAC

The little kittens above (95) have been bred by Mrs Lidyard, and they too are examples of a man-made breed, and one which we shall doubtless see more of in the future. They have self-coloured lilac coats and foreign type, but, as yet have no set standard.

Siamese

Siamese cats were introduced into this country in 1884, being first known as the Royal Cats of Siam, as it is said they were a personal gift from the Royal Palace there. Others followed, but were mostly pets of the wealthy and famous. The Duke of Wellington owned one.

It is strange that in the comparatively short period of 85 years they have flourished to such an extent that they are the most popular of all pedigree cats. From Britain they have been exported all over the world. I wonder what the breeder who wrote the following at the beginning of the century would now think: 'One of the most beautiful of the Short-haired cats is undoubtedly the royal cat of Siam, and the breed is greatly increasing in popularity; but it is never likely to be common, as the cats are delicate in this country.'

The early arrivals did prove to be delicate. The climate was a great change to that to which they had been accustomed, and their owners treated them like hot-house flowers. Having no immunity to the various cat ills in Britain, at first they died like flies, some breeders losing almost their entire catteries following a Show.

Siamese certainly like warmth more than the Long-hairs. My own Long-hairs will never sit close to the fire, as the Siamese do. Even when the snow is on the ground, they will be out catching the snowflakes, not in the least troubled by the cold, but then their coats are more than four inches long. Siamese like their comforts, and it is as well to keep young kittens in an even warmth. One kitten I know sleeps every night on a warm hot-water bottle in a doll's pram, and refuses to go into the pram until his hot-water bottle is there. But Siamese are not delicate cats if brought up correctly, and reared from strong healthy stock, nor is it necessary to keep them in over-heated rooms.

They are the most vociferous of cats. They believe in letting their owners

132

know if they need anything, and will carry on conversations to make their wants known. They answer when spoken to, and have a definite vocabulary which their owners understand.

They are most intelligent cats. I know of one which will open the refrigerator door, even when tied up with string, and get a whole joint out. They love travelling, take readily to a lead, like human companionship, and dislike being left on their own for long periods. If one has to be out all day, it is better to have two kittens to keep one another company, but remember young kittens need feeding during the day.

SEAL-POINTED SIAMESE

The original Siamese in this country were Seal-points, that is they had cream body colouring, and points of a definite seal brown. As time went on, it was realised that it was possible to keep the Siamese coat pattern, but to vary the points colouring. All Siamese are of the Foreign variety, that is they should have long svelte bodies, on slim legs, with the back legs being a little higher than the front ones, and long tapering tails, usually referred to as whip-like. The heads are wedge-shaped, but should never be too round or pointed. The large ears are wide at the base. The oriental-shaped eyes should slant towards the nose, and be a brilliant deep blue.

The first Siamese, as seen in old photographs, were 'apple-headed' rather like the charming, but old-fashioned little lady featured in figure 97. Compare her with the Seal-points in figures 98–9, and the 'new look' may be clearly seen. Mrs Kite's Seal-point (98) believes in helping herself to the milk, while Mrs Hann's Redleaf Benni (99) is now a very worthy champion.

Siamese kittens are almost white when born, and it is several days before the points colouring starts to appear. All Siamese kittens are forward compared with many other varieties, and in a very short time will be clambering over the sides of their basket, rushing around with their little tails held straight up and getting into every mischief imaginable.

133

CHOCOLATE-POINTED SIAMESE

These are most attractive cats with their ivory body colouring, and points the colour of milk chocolate. They are as old a variety as the original Seal-points, but have never been bred in such numbers. It was many years before they were granted a separate breed number. The general characteristics are the same as for all Siamese, the only difference being the body and points colouring.

All Siamese have terrific personalities, and are usually most definite in their likes and dislikes. They are great climbers, and must be taught when quite young not to climb up the curtains and furniture. They love being played with, and many have favourite toys. I have heard of one which has a very small teddy bear that he takes to bed with him every night, snuggling up to it, and talking to it, as if it were another cat. They make good companions, having a great sense of fun. They make excellent pets for children, providing the child is not too young, and has been taught how to hold the kitten, never to squeeze it, and to respect its privacy when it wishes to sleep.

Solitaire Beryl bred by Mrs A. Sayer (100) is justly proud of her Chocolate-point litter. The points colouring is just appearing on the faces.

101 *Tallahassi Biona, a Blue-point*

BLUE-POINTED SIAMESE

The body colouring of this variety should be glacial white gradually shading into blue on the back. The points should be blue. They were once known as 'sports' and one of the early cat fanciers said that 'they would never equal the beauty of the Seal-points and she could see no great object in trying to breed them'. I think she would be most surprised now to see how well the classes are filled at the shows. The characteristics are as for all Siamese, but sometimes this variety is a little on the heavy side.

Siamese develop more rapidly than most other breeds, and many are very precocious. Some females may start calling, that is coming into season, when only five months old, and this is much too early an age for them to start having kittens, so they should be well guarded, and kept well away from any hopeful males. The noise a small Siamese female queen can make is quite incredible, so beware if you live in a flat: the neighbours will probably accuse you of beating your child. If there is no intention of breeding from a female Siamese, spaying is advisable.

Tallahassi Biona, pictured above, has good-shaped ears, a wonderful set of whiskers, and is very proud of her glacial white coat.

Mrs Sayer's Chocolate-point with litter

LILAC-POINTED SIAMESE

These were known in the States for many years, but were not seen in England until 1955, when the first litter were born from Blue-point parentage.

The standard is as for the other Siamese, but the whole appearance is of a lighter-coloured cat, and for this reason the Lilac has an even more oriental look than a great many other 'Foreign' cats.

The body colour should be off-white, almost magnolia, with delicately coloured points of pinkish-grey colour. The pads of the paws and the nose leather are a faded lilac colour. The colouring and the vivid blue almond-shaped eyes add up to a most attractive creature. It has proved immensely popular, and is appearing in ever increasing numbers at the Shows.

The pair bred by Mrs Kite featured above illustrates well their great appeal, as does the litter bred by Mrs E. Fisher (105). Figures 103–4 show Lilac-points in typical Siamese poses. A paper bag will provide fun for hours—and when one is tired out, one can always sleep on mother.

106 *A beautiful Siamese he*

104 *Mrs Appleby's Sleeping Lilac-point*

105 *Mrs Fisher's Lilac-point kittens*

TABBY-POINTED SIAMESE

Siamese with tabby markings had cropped up by chance over the years and were much liked, but it was only comparatively recently that breeders realised that they could be produced to order. Carefully planned matings of Siamese with Silver Tabby Short-hairs produced outstanding animals, but a definite breeding programme was necessary to ensure that these cats with striped points would breed true.

This planned breeding produced outstandingly strong healthy cats, typically Siamese in outline and in character, with long well-proportioned heads and long svelte bodies. The tabby markings give a piquant look to the masks, and this no doubt accounts a great deal for their ever-increasing popularity.

The mask should have clearly defined stripes, particularly around the eyes and the nose. The standard says there should be distinct markings on the cheeks, and the whisker pads darkly spotted. These characteristics may be seen well in the picture of Mrs Pears' Tabby-points with her Tabby and Seal-point kittens. The legs should have varying-sized broken stripes, with solid markings on back, the tail being ringed and ending in a solid tip. The ears should be almost thumb-marked with black, and the brilliant clear blue oriental-shaped eyes should be black-rimmed.

Some people are sorry that efforts are being made to breed out the kinks in the tails of all Siamese, although a slight kink at the extremity is still permitted. Legend has it that the first kinks appeared when the Royal Princesses in Siam used their cats' tails as ring holders while they swam in the river, and the tails bent over to stop the rings falling off. Other Siamese lovers decry the loss of the squint. This is still occasionally seen, but is not now encouraged by breeders.

The coat of all the Siamese varieties, whatever the points colouring, should be very short and fine in texture, glossy and close-lying. Grooming is no problem. Light brushing and combing is sufficient. It should never be too hard, otherwise all the undercoat will be brushed out. Hard stroking with the hand gives the coat a natural gloss. As in all cats, condition is important, but loss of it seems to show up very quickly in the Siamese. The fur opens, the masks becomes brindled, and the haws may be seen.

Feeding is much the same as for other cats, but do beware, if you have a new

144

107   Mrs Pear's Tabby and Seal-point Siamese

kitten, not to overdo the cow's milk until you are sure he can tolerate it, and give just a little at a time. In fact, some Siamese dislike it altogether and much prefer water at all times.

108   Mrs Pear's Tabby and Seal–point kittens

109 *Siamese at play*

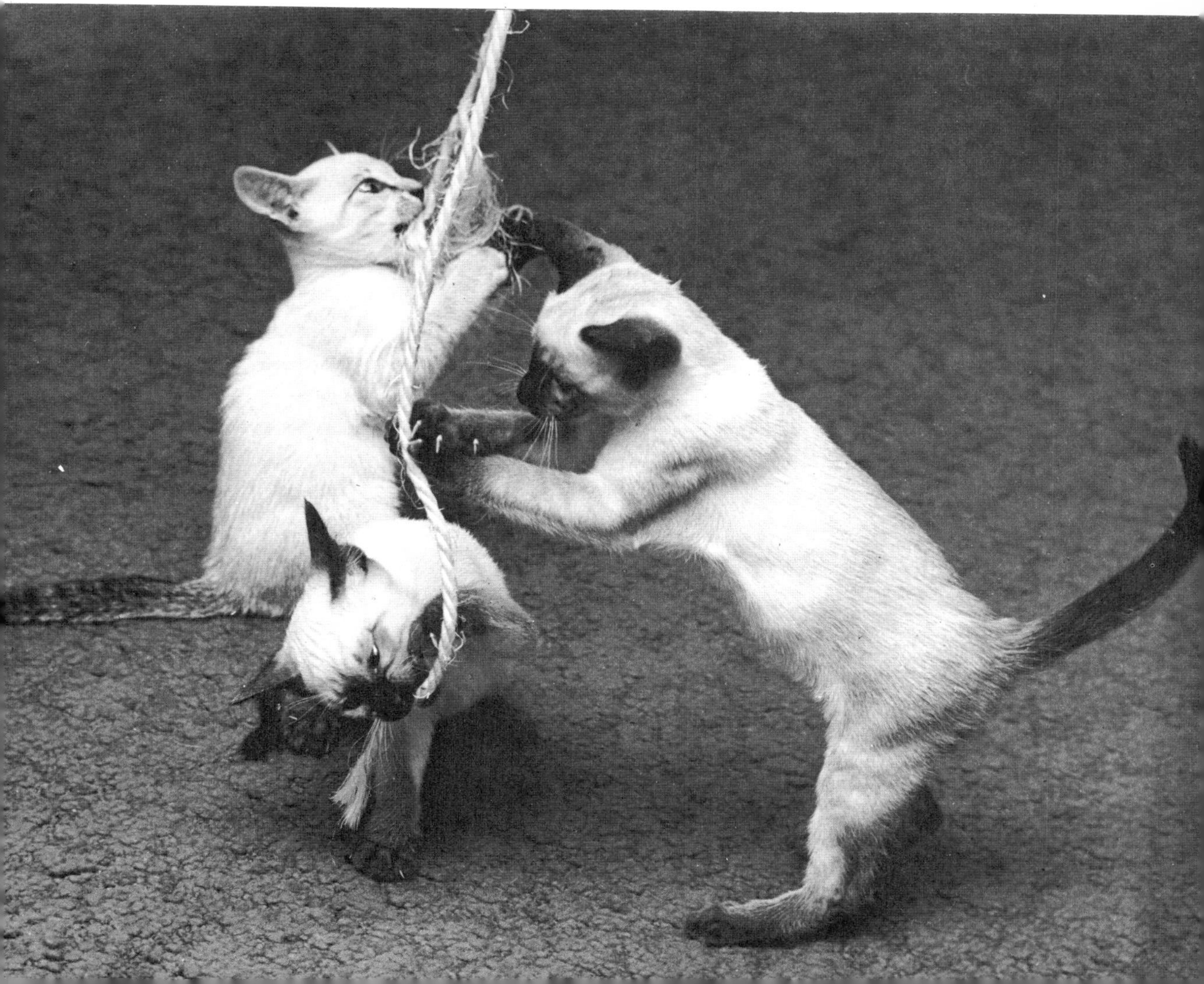

RED-POINTED SIAMESE

This variety has been known for many years, having been produced by selective breeding, but has only recently been given a breed number. They are distinctive cats, typically Siamese, with a body colouring of white shading to apricot on the back, the points being of a bright reddish gold. The points colouring should be pure, and there should be no tabby markings on the face. Rings still appear on the tail, which are proving difficult to breed out.

Solitaire Cinnibar bred by Mrs Sayers (110) is a Red-point used to being photographed, and accepts admiration as a matter of course.

TORTIE-POINT SIAMESE

This is a fairly new variety, and is very striking as may be seen from the photograph of Mrs Chapman's Peekslane Southview Astrid (111). The body colour should be cream or fawn, with the ears seal colour with red and the points being marbled with seal, cream, and a little red. Tortie-points are female only, and according to the stud used will produce an interesting selection of kittens, some of which may possibly be male Red-points.

ANY OTHER COLOUR SIAMESE

As well as the point colourings already mentioned, it has also been found possible to produce Siamese with other point colourings, such as Cream, Blue Cream, Chocolate Cream and Lilac Cream. There are as yet no set standards for these variations, so they cannot compete for challenge certificates.

111   *Peckslane Southview Astrid, a Tortie-point*

SIAMESE KITTENS

Siamese kittens develop at an early age, and if you have a male kitten it is advisable to have him neutered when about $3\frac{1}{2}$ months old. The vet will advise you as to if he considers it the correct age for your kitten. Over the age of 6 months, an anaesthetic is compulsory by law, but whatever the age most owners prefer that one should be given. Very little ill effect should be

150

felt, and by the evening the kitten is usually as lively as ever, not even going off his food. He should not be fed before having an anaesthetic, so will probably be very hungry by the evening, but only light food should be given then.

If not neutered, a young male will probably start spraying around the house, leaving his most pungent smell around him, and may take to wandering far from home to find a female cat.

I have mentioned female kittens elsewhere, but would like to repeat that, if you do buy a female kitten, and do not have her spayed, beware the local toms. When she comes into season, they will probably know long before you do, and if you have no wish to hear the patter of many tiny kitten feet around the house, suitable precautions must be taken. Many calling queens are escapists, and can get through incredibly small holes, when they have the urge.

When introducing a new kitten to your home, remember that Siamese are the most inquisitive of all creatures, and please make sure that the fire is well-guarded. He may have been used to central heating, and may choose to explore the chimney. I have known this happen more than once. Remember too to close the windows, as a kitten can squeeze through a very small space. When he first arrives, it is better to sit quietly with him in one room, and let him explore on his own. I think it is advisable to have a toilet tray on some newspaper in a corner, as if he has travelled a long way, he may need to use it. At first, he will smell at all the strange furniture, and probably retreat at the slightest noise to the nearest hiding place, under the settee or the sideboard. But in time, if left alone, he will come up, and before you know where you are will be demanding to sit on your lap.

For the first night at least give him a basket or cardboard box, with a warm hot-water bottle covered with a blanket, as he will miss the warmth of his mother and the other kittens. But, more often than not, he will probably finish up asleep on your bed!

Pet cats

This heading is perhaps a little misleading, as the majority of all domestic cats, whether pedigree or mongrel, are kept as pets. As organiser of a large Cat Show, mainly for pedigree cats, but with a separate section for pet cats, I get many letters from children, saying that their cat is pedigree, but, of course, is also their pet, so which section do they enter him in. This can be very puzzling for a child.

The term 'pet cat' is taken as referring to one whose mother was of indefinite parentage, and whose father was probably not even known, in other words a mongrel. Mongrel or not, these kittens can be delightful, are usually highly intelligent, and very responsive to any love and attention given them. They may have long noses and green eyes, with coat colours and patterns unlike those of the registered varieties, but they are still very photogenic, as may be seen by the charming photographs (112–13) overleaf.

According to the pet food manufacturers, there has over recent years been a decrease in the numbers of pet cats, and an increase in the pedigree. Neutering and spaying may be causing the decrease in the pets. Sometimes it proves quite difficult even to find a pet kitten.

The best thing is to get one from a neighbour, as you will then know the home from which it comes, and be sure that it is sturdy and healthy. The various Animal Welfare Societies often have kittens for which they are seeking good homes, or even older cats, whose owners for some reason or other are unable to keep them. Most people set their hearts on having a young kitten, but taking an older cat can be quite rewarding. A little more patience may be needed to allow the cat to settle down in strange surroundings. It will probably be house-trained, be easier to feed, and as many of the older cats have to be destroyed for lack of suitable homes, you will have saved its life.

As I mentioned right at the beginning, do remember to have a kitten innoculated against Feline Infectious Enteritis, and keep it away from other cats or kittens until this has been done This is a killer disease with a high mortality rate.

Pets need just as much general care as any pedigree cat. In fact, there is no difference. All should be groomed, and their ears and eyes kept clean. I find many pet owners look after their cats' coats beautifully, but entirely forget the ears, and are dismayed if their pets are turned down by the vet for this reason when entered for a Show.

The pets featured in figures 114–15 are in beautiful condition, and would, I am sure, win prizes at any Pet Cat Show.

112, 113,
Pet kittens

114 *The household pet*

*Mrs S.
ghes' Atabbi*

Index

Note: Numerals in heavy type refer to the figure numbers of the illustrations.